Tea Time With Jesus

Words of Encouragement

From A Woman's Heart to A Woman's Soul

Laura Taeko Sanders

Copyright © 2008 Laura Taeko Sanders

ISBN: 978-1-60383-058-4

Published by:
Holy Fire Publishing
Unit 116
1525-D Old Trolley Rd.
Summerville, SC 29485

www.ChristianPublish.com

Cover Design: Jay Cookingham

Printed in the United States of America and the United Kingdom

ACKNOWLEDGMENTS

My Heart's Deepest 'Thank You'

This book was possible because of you...

To New Hope Church at Oahu and Leeward, and our Senior Pastor, Dr. Wayne Cordeiro. You introduced life journaling to my husband. My husband then shared this gem with me and we imprinted this treasure to our children and to theirs. To New Hope Windward, our home church, and our Senior Pastor, Dave Barr and Lisa (his wife and my friend) -you're God-sent.

To my husband Marcus, my sons Chris and Tim, Ashley Matsuura, Sarah Bartolome, and Dawn O' Brien for jumping in to share your gift given to you by God, a gift of writing. Thank You for your thorough job in proofing my rough manuscript and honing it so excellently.

To my Family: My husband, Marcus, you believed in me from the very beginning to the very finish. You stood by my side through it all. And to our three precious children-Christopher, Timothy, and Janell-you sacrificed behind the scenes where only God saw.

And especially to the One Whom I owe the reason and existence of this book made possible. To my God, a special "thank you".

Reflect on Tea Time With Jesus...

Table Of Contents

Reflect on Tea Time With Jesus...

GOD'S PERFECT TIMING,

TEA TIME WITH JESUS

…"at just the right time, when we were still powerless,
Christ died for the ungodly." (Romans 5:6)

*P*owerless. Does this mean when we are bound by chains and find we have no strength to defeat our enemies? *Yes.* Or is it when we run a marathon and feel absolutely without stamina as we near the finish line? *Yes.* How about the times we face our toughest crossroads? *Yes.* Powerless is all of the above and even when our hearts loose

7

the hope to carry on. Then we are definitely powerless with a capital 'P'!

I am grateful beyond measure because when I was 'powerless' God lavished me with His abounding mercy. In spite of my weaknesses, with His life, He overcame the sting of death. Not that I even deserved it. It was because God loved me so much. He loves (present and on-going). His love saved my powerlessness, my hopelessness. When I was blinded, God gave me sight. He loved enough to turn my ashes into beauty, His beauty from inside out. God lifted my countenance, put a smile on my face, and gave me a skip in my walk; all at just the right time.

God's timing is perfect. He has given this day set before me to spend, only 24 hours. Do I use it foolishly and on my own strength? *Powerless.* Or do I live it whole-heartedly depend on God with nothing held back? **Powerful**. Then how can I be powerful for Jesus? Here is the key: My quiet Time with God (Tea Time). Everyday, for each day is a new beginning. The hours of yesterday are gone and spent. The hours of tomorrow are yet to come and may not even come.

So now, now is the time. Make it count. Live it with God's power.

So here's the 'how-to' make life count powerfully: Spend time with God before diving into the day's non-ending busy demands. Pray. Being still and hearing God for wise directions will definitely help calm us from running too fast in the power-packed day. It helps to seize life packed with power in the right time, God's timing. When we live life in this powerful way, each moment will count with the very best God desires to shower His children with. This helps us to have less regrets when all is said and done.

Now, take a second and ask this prayer… Thank you, my God, for this powerful reminder. Yes, Your directions become clear as I spend more time, prime time with You. ***Powerful.*** This is what I am determined to do, please give me the strength to put this priceless gem into action. My heart desires this-I love Tea Time with You.

Reflect on Tea Time With Jesus...

SPOTLESS CLOSETS

..."Son of man, have you seen what the elders of the house of Israel

are doing in the darkness, each at the shrine of his own idol?

They say, 'The Lord does not see us..." (Ezekiel 8:12)

D o we put on our Sunday-best only in front of the public eye, out in the open before the witnesses of people? Yet, when we let down our hair and reveal our behind-the-scenes' closet spaces, are they full of skeletons? Well, the leaders in the house of Israel did so. They led during the daylight at God's house. The elders did their jobs before God's people. Still in their dark secret times, they

11

forsook God and broke His heart big time. They thought that no one saw, not even the Lord. They missed it.

Realize we are presently living in the day and age of God's grace for the Church. So all the more, our quiet closet spaces should be one of the most precious areas. These places can be in our car as we drive to and from our destinations. It can be right next to our bedside where our carpets have the imprint of our bended knees. For me, it is at the foot of our stairway leading up to our loft where my husband's study room is. It is here my husband finds his well before the dry deserts. In the loft is where he hears the instructions given directly from the Master Teacher Himself for the day and for each day to follow. At the foot of this place, before the birds greet their Song Writer with their voices, I sit at my Lord's Feet. This is a special place where my heart first beats at the break of dawn, and this is where I end the last breath of each day.

When we choose to put our priorities in such order, there is nothing to be kept secret in the quiet closets. Our closet corners are spotless. So when God looks to and from this earth in search of His faithful ones…we do not have to be ashamed.

*May this be your heartbeat also…*In the open, Lord, I devote my entire life a fresh and anew. This means in every corner of my closet, search and clean it. I give You full permission to do what ever it takes until it is spotless clean. Then I am sure when You call me by name, I can say "Here I am, Lord" with joy.

Reflect on Tea Time With Jesus...

PICTURE PERFECT

Even in darkness light dawns for the upright, for the gracious and compassionate and righteous man. (Psalm 112:4)

Picture this...a cozy pinewood exterior, log-cabin like home nestled in the middle of a gated Christian community, bedded amidst God's mountain. Outside, the climate is freezing cold and already glistening with soft snowflakes. Inside, the temperature is just perfect with the fireplace warming the home at the thermostat setting of 72 degrees. In the family room, children are laughing and playing, and content parents are sitting back in the loveseat taking to heart this Kodak moment. On one side of this room

15

stretches a large glass window looking over the outspread of the beautiful view. Night has set in, and the moon casts a glow throughout the vast forestry, making visibility possible. What an ideal ambiance, what a perfect picture.

Today, as we walk our day to day journey on this temporary home of ours called Earth, we get to enjoy snapshots of such a scenario. Yet, amidst all this beauty, rain and storm are also included as part of the whole package called life. Life is not always this picture perfect. Still, we do not have to be afraid. God promises "even in darkness light dawns for the upright, for the gracious and compassionate man and woman, young or old".

The key to capturing the heart of this life verse is to "live right before God and fellow men". This means not only out in the open where we are visible for others to see, but more so behind closed doors. In our quiet closet corners where only God sees, we must be true and honest with all our masks laid down, and with our heart's motives exposed wide. You see, even if our God sees right through every hidden motive nestled deep within our hearts, God loves when His children trusts Him enough to Ask Him. So when real times of less-then-picture-perfect circumstances arise, when push comes to shove, we must choose to stumble on the side of righteousness. Also, if we allow God permission to, He will be the Great Light that can pierce right through the darkness. He will delight in helping us, only if we allow Him to.

*Here's a prayer to ponder on...*Dearest Lord, I need Your strength to do what I must. It's a little easier done Sunday mornings when I stand in front of Your people to minister. But, in the quiet closet times when I'm less then perfect, I am asking Your truth and grace to shine in spite of me. Also I ask, "Please, when life is less than picture perfect and I cannot see clearly, cast Your light so visibility is possible".

Reflect on Tea Time With Jesus...

NOW

Take warning… To whom can I speak and give warning?

Who will listen to me? But I gave them this command:

Obey me, and I will be your God and you will be my people.

Walk in all the ways I command you that it may go well with you.

(Jeremiah 6:8,10,23)

Last night, one of my man-o-pause moments hit. I said some unwise choices of words to my husband. I know this had saddened his heart, and this had definitely broken God's. I also felt so broken and chose to lie down in our bed. I laid silently for a few moments. Before I could count one sheep, I was fast asleep. Then in the middle of the night, God woke me up. He gave me clear directions to follow, *now*. The directions were simply a requirement on my part to say, "I'm sorry". The choice was in my court now. *Will I choose to allow the enemy a footstool and play day in our unity as husband and wife? No!* So I immediately mustered up all the faith I had in the moment and asked, "Lord, please give me your strength to say what I must...just please let my husband be awake." The awesome moments that followed in the middle of the night went like this-I gingerly asked my husband if he was awake. His answer was "Yes". I was then able to obey God's directions and apologize from my heart with these spoken words, "I am so sorry, honey." All was sweetly well after this powerful step.

With this, I gained an unforgettable life gem...when God speaks the very first time, 'Listen and obey'. The result will be God's will, His miracles. So quickly listen without struggling and take every ounce of your might to obey. You will be a Winner!

*Let this prayer be yours today...*Abba Father, thank you for being patient with me. Even when I fall short, Your faithfulness lifts me high above my momentary struggles. Whenever I stumble and become like a little child in my childish ways, remind me to take one little baby step forwards, *now*. You will honor this act of obedience and carry me all the way to the final miracle orchestrated just by You.

Reflect on Tea Time With Jesus...

LISTEN TO THE KNOCK

Samuel said to Saul, "I am the one the Lord sent to anoint you king over His people Israel; so listen now to the message from the Lord."

(1 Samuel 15:1)

How many lessons and gems does it take for us to finally be willing to receive God's instructions? How many quiet reminders do we need from God himself before we let go of our own agendas and let God's Will be done? Samuel's message from God to Saul was this-"Now go, attack the Amalekites and totally destroy everything that belongs to them. Do not spare them..."

"But Saul and his army spared Agag and the best of the sheep and cattle..."everything that was good in order to sacrifice them to the Lord God. The Bible says that Saul was unwilling to carry out God's instructions fully. This broke God's Heart. This also caused Saul to run his life course off the race eventually, and to miss out on God's plan of hope and a future. This was God's message through Samuel to Saul-"Does the Lord delight in sacrifices as much as in obedience to the voice of God? It is better to obey than to sacrifice."

As God's children, we are the apple of His Eyes. We were the reason He paid the priceless price on the Cross many years ago. We are His voice to our mission fields (in our own home, at our jobs, as we walk around the shopping malls filled with people created as such). The hope we know through Jesus is in our hands to be shared. We are the messengers of His Love extended through kind words, kind actions, and kindness generously and unconditionally given. But there is something far more precious then any righteous actions we can give or say. When all is said and all is done here on earth, *'did we do it God's way?'*

Well, here's a story that may help clarify this important question. I am a piano teacher and my students are practicing countless hours in preparation towards a Spring Piano Recital. Meanwhile, as they come to each lesson, I give out a grade of an A, B, or C. Just prior to the recital, those who have faithfully accomplished A's will be awarded trophies. How will they grasp the A's? By simply following the instructions I lay out for them lesson by lesson. Such as:

1. Perfect notes for the measures assigned-33pts.
2. Master its counting and rhythm-33pts.
3. Dynamics- 33pts.
4. Follow these instructions-1 pt. bonus.

Interestingly, I just gave a small talk on a lesson concerning the value of following instructions. A student came back. He had practiced his heart out for the week. He had mastered steps #1 and #2, but totally ignored instruction #3. This cost him, from a possible A grade to a Failing grade.

So, does it pay off to follow God's directions? Definitely!

Reflect on Tea Time With Jesus...

TUG OF WAR

Ps. 60:12 With God we will gain the victory...

My strength or God's?(Psalm 60:12)

Last Christmas, our daughter Janell, gave a wonderful gift to our two dogs. It was a toy that was shaped like a rope. They both loved it, especially our Golden Retriever, Mele. If Mele could speak, I'm sure this is what she will say..."*Yes, my Family is here! Let me bring this new toy to them.*" We of course pay attention to her joy and we play the famous game called Tug of War. This fills her tank, and her age seems to melt away till she acts just like a puppy. Sometimes we jerk it to give her a little challenge. Sometimes we give her a chance to win to tickle her endorphins. Sometimes she generously allows us the victory. It's a give and take-we give graciously and we take away joy from it.

In life, I am approaching my autumn years. With this season, I get to taste the real flavor of the game of Tug of War. I must admit, it's one of the toughest yet most blessed season I have ever experienced. Toughest, because to win I must pull harder and my submissive little girl gets lost in the midst. It's a constant battle, 24-7. But through this, God has passed on to me a life line-a gem to pull me through.

Here is the gem: God desires to be strong in our lives (the Champion of Tug-of-Wars). He wants to do miracles both small and big. In order to do so, a need must arise. When this need comes our way, instead of asking, "How do I get out of it," ask "How do I get through this?"

*See if this prayer hits home with you...*Here I am. I let go of my agendas, my worries. To go through this season means not my will but Yours. My human self would love to run away and hide. Yet You have another plan, the perfect plan.

Please help my baby steps to be steady as I take Your faith in my right pocket and look up as I take this journey through this mountain. It's the tallest I've ever seen, from my standpoint, I cannot even see the top of it. I feel so inadequate and the Tug of War calls on me so loudly: *My strength or Yours*, God? Be the Winner at this Tug of War, be my Champion. I will be more than content to be second place.

Reflect on Tea Time With Jesus...

IN YOUR EMBRACE

Finally, be strong in the Lord and in His mighty power. Put on the full armor of God so that you can take your stand against the devil's schemes. For our struggle is not against flesh and blood, but against …the power of this dark world. (Ephesians 6:10-12)

I knocked at my Father's door early this morning.
I had nothing but my brokenness to offer.
Do you know what He gave me in return?
In return, I received comforting Peace.
I stood in front of my life-sized mirror.
Its reflection only showed ashes.

31

God exchanged it for beauty instead.

I looked through my window and couldn't see beyond the confusion of the storm clouds. Instead, I received solid directions and perfect answers to my questions.

I drove passed the Ko'olau Range. As far as the eyes beheld, mountains overwhelmed my human vision.
Then my eyes caught the view of oceans spread out in quiet stillness as a backdrop of God's provision for me. God reminded me how still He had set it for me so I could walk on it, just like Jesus had shown me how to do.

As I waited for God's audience through the stillness, He let me know: It was not by my strength or my might. It was by a crucial answer I found at His Feet this morning...I found God's Grace, so strong and so gracious, I was in His embrace.

BRIDGE of SECOND CHANCES

...I do not consider myself yet to have taken hold of it.
But one thing I do: Forgetting what is behind and straining toward
what is ahead. (Philippians 3:13)

We journey down the long, narrow, winding road of life. We pass through the corridors with so many doors all around us. This makes poor decisions unavoidable at times. In the weakness of this moment, we may fall prey to sin. It may be big or small, out in the open or hidden. Either way, what should we do?

Do we stay down, or do we keep fighting forwards? Philippians 3:13 speaks loud and clear: Forget what fumbles and mistakes we have made. Fretting about it will not change anything. Instead, what we do about it will make a difference in changing the course of history. So when we fall flat on our faces, don't stay down. Get up on your knees and ask God. Ask Him for a pass to the 'bridge of second chances'.

Here you'll find answers of hope. Here you'll find hosts of counselors to surround you and cheer you back on track. Especially, here you'll find a loving Father's arms aching to embrace you with unconditional love.

*Take a glance and soak this in...*we are the most blessed bunch of kids. We are God's kids who have access 24-7 to the greatest Father ever. In this world, it is rare to find second chances. But our God is the Author of it. God authors each of His children to the unlimited pass to enter the Bridge of Second Chances.

PAY CLOSE ATTENTION

We must pay more careful attention, therefore, to what we have heard, so that we do not drift away. (Hebrews 2:1)

We as human beings get to 'learn'. It's just part of life here on earth. In many of the lessons we learn, we have a choice of the method by which we learn it. One way, which is shied away from most, is called 'learning through pain'. Now pain is something even I would rather stay far away from.

So here is a story that will tickle your thoughts and will drive home the gem...I can recall over four decades ago, I chose unwise words to say to my father and then reaped just payment. My godly Christian father did what he must. He pulled out his thick buckled belt that was wrapped around his waist moments prior. The use was absolutely Biblical – don't spare the rod or you'll spoil the child. On my part, the impression of pain remains with me as a remembrance and a lifelong lesson. Then as time passed and I was a few years riper, I remember asking my mother, "Why don't I get any more spankings?" My mother's reply was simply, "Because you have learned to listen well."

Now, everyone has a different level of receiving pain. In other words, some may be able to tolerate more punishment and still come back fighting. But as for me, a small degree of pain gets my attention at a heartbeat. For I know as a living testimony: *without pain, there is no gain.* So with 'pain' as our teacher, and Jesus by our side, we are indeed set up for success.

R.S.V.P. IS URGENT

...Let me inherit a double portion of your spirit... (2 Kings 2:9)

Here are three life questions:

1. Have you been traveling down life's lane on auto-drive and feeling like you've been trucking down the seasons a long, long time and you're beyond caution?

2. Now, if you took a careful look, or have you become tired and a bit sloppy around the seams?

3. Lately, has God been loving you through a Father's tough love hoping to catch your attention?

If your answers to any of these questions are "yes", here's the answer to your answers...First, catch this-'*Time is of the essence*'. Remember, Elijah did ask Elisha if there was anything he could do for him before God came to call him home? At that moment, Elisha's reply was not for anything specific but everything that mattered the most. "Give me a double portion of your spirit" is what he asked for. So like Elisha, we too must act immediately. For R.S.V.P. is urgent. Now is the time, before you take another step towards your actions. So we too can ask God for a double portion of His Spirit. This means for:

- His wisdom to see beyond anything that stops you from moving forwards.
- His strength to overcome what you are facing.
- His heart to love others even if they have hurt you.
- Forgiveness towards yourself. Do not allow the devil (your real enemy) to eat away at your joy any longer. Do not beat yourself up for being human.

*Here's a woman's vulnerable prayer...*Here is my R.S.V.P. because You, my God, are on the other end eager to respond to my response. Life in June has been one of the toughest ever to go through. There have been many high hurdles to overcome, many crucial decisions to make, and some huge giants to tackle. But because You gave me the wisdom to R.S.V.P., I cried out to You, and You attended to my cry immediately. Now, my heart is excited. I found new hope in You. You drew back the darkness and allowed morning to break through. I see the reality of Your answers to my questions vividly. Now, I receive Your awesome joy for our entire household…

Reflect on Tea Time With Jesus...

JOY COMES IN THE MORNING

This is what the Lord Almighty says: "Just as I had determined to bring disaster upon you and showed no pity when your fathers angered me,"..."so now I have determined to do good again... The fasts will become joyful..." (Zechariah 8:14,15,19)

Have the pains and the bruises caused by the day to day push and shove pushed you to check out of life for a season? For a short while I did too. I merely existed and did what was required of me, nothing more nothing less. The joy of life itself took a backseat, and the difficulties accentuated. Then in my desperate emptiness, I cried out "help!" to God. He heard me. In lightning speed He came to my rescue. What shape did my help come in? Well, it came in the package shaped as a broken heart. God knew and cared very much for me. He knew I needed to be broken before I could be built up and restored once again.

Through this I've gained a priceless golden nugget...How can healing be needed if there isn't a wound first? So here's the great news-desperate storm times will not last forever. Joy comes in the morning. As Zechariah speaks of God's promise after the storm, after the heartaches, after the mourning, healing and joy of a new morning awaits.

*Ponder on this...*God's Word of encouragement to you and to me is to keep moving forwards. Do not lose courage. God yearns to grab hold of our steering wheels. Our next destination is waiting to enjoy in His luscious vineyard. Here, we can take joy in harvesting a refreshing swim in an oasis of a hope-filled victory garden. "When will this be?" I asked. God answered, "Joy comes in the morning just around the river bend."

GOLDEN DAYS

Compared to Job, did I wake up with my body plagued by sores and exposed to the harsh outside weather? Instead, I woke up this beautiful morning in our comfortable bed, surrounded by soft pillows and my husband's arms. I found myself to be content and healthy with the only exception of a few blemishes to flaw my face.

Like the widow and two sons Elisha prayed for, did I go to sleep on an empty stomach that ached with hunger pains? Do I dream of a small morsel of food to satisfy the emptiness? Instead, I am wonderfully blessed to have three home-cooked meals for our entire household to enjoy.

Do I go about this day in desperation and hopelessness, such as in the days of Saul, later known as Paul, when the pressure on the Church was intense? Instead, I have the joy and fulfillment of knowing whatever I face today, my God is with me.

Am I a slave driven under a cruel dictatorship as were the children of Israel in the days of Egypt? Instead, today, I get to enjoy freedom. I can feel safe to sit in an open public and pray with family and friends, read the Bible, if I please. We can even have church openly in school auditoriums and even in theatres.

Sometimes I may loose sight of how blessed I really am. But when I do, I must remember: There are a million others who are less fortunate then me-widows and orphans, prisoners and captives... (Now this is what the Lord Almighty says) "Give careful thought to your ways. You have planted much, but have harvested little" ...Why...Because of my house, which

remains in ruin, while each of you is busy with his own house.
(Haggai 1:5,6,9)

Are we sometimes so caught up in making ends meet that it becomes the ends to a means? In the process, are we falling short in doing our real mission for such a time as this? In the book of Haggai, God speaks volume. So many today are busy. Busy trying to make a living:

Wake up in the wee hours.
Grab a bite on the run.
Spend precious moments just to make a few dollars.
Forget about lunch.
It's almost time to sleep.
I better head on home. Come home.
What does my little girl look like?
How tall are my boys?
What did my wife's dinner taste like?
Where did all the years go?

God says, come alive. Do you remember why you are placed here for such a time as this? You cannot buy time, it's too valuable. You cannot redo passed moments, they fly by in a blink.

Then don't get so caught up in dying while trying to make ends meet. God is still waiting. He is patient and the Gentleman of all gentlemen. He will not force His great plan on you. He will gingerly step aside until you are finished tossing and turning in the lesser things. Then you are ready to begin what you are really called to do in this season of life. Then and only then, everything will become truly fulfilling and meaningful. Just the way God intended for His precious children's days here on earth to be. Our days are meant to be spent for eternal, kingdom-difference reasons.

Get up! Drop all unnecessary weights. Step forward in sync with God. Don't waste anymore once-in-a-lifetime Golden opportunities.

BABY COUNTENANCE

I lift up my eyes to you, to you whose throne is in heaven. As the eyes of slaves look to the hand of their master, as the eyes of a maid look to her mistress, so our eyes look to the Lord, our God, till he shows us his mercy. (Psalm 123:1,2)

Did you take notice of how eyes mirror the expression of the heart? Little children are the best models of this. They sincerely express the honesty of how they feel in the moment. When they feel sad or happy, upset or calm, you can look into their eyes and immediately know how they feel deep within.

I remember when our son, Chris, was about a year and a half. We went shopping, a day out as a family. We strolled our son in his baby buggy. Took him to his favorite section (the Toyland) and let him hold onto a soft, cuddly stuffed animal. But he was besides his usual cheerful self that day. His eyes told the whole story-he was under the weather, he was not feeling well.

In life, we have days where we too stumble and fall short. There are days where we may be besides our normal selves. We may loose courage in facing our giants. We may loose strength to keep pushing on. But when and if we do stumble and fall short in pleasing God, all we need to do is explained clearly in today's verse...all we must do is to look up to heaven and fall onto our knees.

Pray with a pure childlike heart and a baby countenance that sincerely desires forgiveness from our Abba Father, our Daddy God. How can our God, who loves us as the apple of His eyes, turn His caring eyes from this? How can He not provide us with even the desires of our hearts?

*Feel this heartbeat...*I lift up my eyes to You, my Abba Father, to Your throne in heaven. As the eyes of a maid look to her mistress, so do my eyes look to You, Lord. I will keep on till I find favor in Your eyes. I will continue till I find Your mercy and grace. I will not give up until I receive the miracle I ask for unspoken at this moment. Until the answer comes, I will knock at Your door so I can testify about Your wonderful faithfulness and others may know too of Your goodness. Until that precious time, with joyful anticipation, I look to You, Abba Father, with a baby countenance.

Reflect on Tea Time With Jesus...

BIG FATHER

Praise the Lord, all you servants of the Lord who minister by night in the house of the Lord. May the Lord, the Maker of heaven and earth, bless you from Zion. (Psalm 134:3)

Here's a something to chew on: *Words can set the imagination wild, a photo sets clear any doubts and puts into vivid perspective the untamed imagination.* Simply put-a photo prints a clear picture for the imagination to grasp and the mind to finally understand.

How true this is. This past weekend I experienced a priceless time that allowed me to testify about this gem. You see, for over four and a half decades I have known Jesus as my Lord and Savior. I could only imagine through the words written in the greatest Book ever published about how awesome my God is. I always believed He was bigger than my biggest fears. But after seeing this weekend's service with my own eyes, via DVD, spoken through Louie Gigglio, something within me sparked and ignited a fresh belief. Clearly, my giants shrunk from being enormous to ant-size. I gained a truly vivid picture of *how* Big God is.

With just a single breath, God spoke the planets and the stars into existence. With just one breath, He breathed life into man and into woman. He breathed life into you and me.

As Big as God is, He visited this earth to face the most horrible death to pay the debt of my sin and yours. He didn't have to, He wanted to because His love was definitely as Big as He is.

After seeing this picture of God's wondrous works, the snapshot of the awesome stars He flung into space without effort, I finally understood. I do not have to worry whether

God can handle my obstacles and tests in life. When I pray a small prayer and ask God for help, there should be no more doubt of how much Bigger God is.

*See with me…*So, with new insight into the Majesty of You, Lord, this beautiful morning, I pen this prayer: I see the sight of Your awesomeness as the morning sun peeks through. The night sky steps aside graciously. I ask with new eyes, Lord. Now I understand more of what your spokesman, T.D. Jakes says-*Do not despise the giants of the dark times.* I feel I must ask a double portion of your Spirit. Please, Abba Father, strengthen my husband and our children. I know You are bigger than any of our giants and are watching over us. So I stand in the gap for our whole household…as a little daughter asks her 'Big Father', I ask for Your strength, wisdom and miracles step by step…*there is no doubt.*

Reflect on Tea Time With Jesus...

HAPPY THANKSGIVING

Praise the Lord...and forget not all his benefits... who satisfies your
desires with good things so that your youth is renewed like the
eagle's. (Psalms 103:2,5)

Make a wish? No, pray instead. God always provides. When your prayer is answered, tender the God-moment and give God praise.

This Thanksgiving Day was especially dear to me-filled with lots of God-moments. It was just like the moment the glass slipper was placed on Cinderella's feet. The fit was to the 'T' and oh so perfect. Her heart must have jumped with joy and contentment in the moment. This Thanksgiving moment, our home was blessed with family and friends. Our tables were topped with such splendor filled with delicious homemade spread of delicacies. Everyone left our home content at the end of the evening because each one had a special part in making the day very memorable. It couldn't have been a more perfect day!

Many times we miss the joys of life because we take too much effort looking for the BIG miracles to fill our tanks. But really, if only we look more carefully, the little but precious miracles are all around us. Why? Because God loves to lavish His children with good things so our youth is renewed like the eagles.

We know life does not always go perfectly. This is a given. Besides, life is so short and we pass through it only once. So let's choose today, to do everything in our power to tender the small yet significant little miracles day in and day out. Then surely at the end of our journey here on earth, we will have a treasure chest full of precious memories to leave as a legacy.

*Savor this moment and consider this...*Dear Abba Father, I lack nothing because You take me by the hand. When the going gets tough and I feel like I cannot hold on anymore, You shower me with strength beyond the moment. You keep me soaring on wings like the eagle's. You allow my youth to be renewed. Now, after five decades, that's Amazing!

Reflect on Tea Time With Jesus...

THE RESCUE

The Lord will have compassion on Jacob; once again he will choose
Israel and will settle them in their own land. (Isaiah 14:1)

This early morn, we rescued a little flinch. She's so sweet, so innocent. This little one is definitely God's masterpiece. It's at the stage where it wants to try out its wings. It can only wobbly flop out of its nest. Yet it's not quite able to fly yet.

I found it being tossed by our two curious dogs, a Golden Retriever and a Chow Chow. So immediately, with my mother's hat on, I moved our dogs aside and carried the little bird into our home. I took it straight to our daughter, Janell, and showed her the surprise that God sent just for her. Janell loves animals so God knew exactly how to fill her tank with joy.

We then decided to place the baby bird into a cozy picnic basket with some soft tissue laid on the bottom for her bedding. After, we consulted our good friends, Sharrel and Mailani for their expertise. They gave us some wise next-steps to take. Janell and I followed the directions exactly and here's the happy climax to this story: Afterwards, we put our dogs in our backyard and let our new found friend gingerly back outside under the shade of our trees. No sooner after we did, my daughter and I stepped back to watch. Do you know what heartwarming event we witnessed?

Well, out of nowhere it seemed, both the mother and father birds arrived. They had heard their baby's "peep" and in a heartbeat came to its rescue. With the best berries in mouth, and a juicy worm too, both parents joined their long lost baby in a happy miracle reunion. And for hours on end, neither parent left. Both took turns in pampering and protecting their priceless little one.

Through this I learned a valuable life gem: If little birds have such love for one another, how much more our God loves us. His love bankrupted heaven. His love took Him the second mile of pain and shame. His love led Him to lay his very life down for His priceless little ones-you and me. Now this defines the meaning of 'Compassion'.

*I challenge you to understand the depth...*Dearest Lord, I take this orchestrated heaven-sent day because You want me to understand the depth of Your love. As Your child, I too stumble and fall time after time, yet your mercy catches me regardless. All the while You patiently stand by my side, watching, cheering me along till I am finally able to soar high above like the eagle. I want to always be reminded of the passion of Your love (especially when I walk through the hard times). When I am reminded of Your love, may I also know You have already proven Your faithfulness to deliver the promise to come to *our Rescue.*

Reflect on Tea Time With Jesus...

21st CENTURY RUTH

...But Ruth replied...where you go I will go, and where you stay I will stay. Your people will be my people and your God my God.

(Ruth 1:16)

The book called Ruth in the Bible can surely be overlooked and missed if we even blinked our eyes. Still if we search carefully, we can find rich nuggets of great worth here. Here we can find a story that will warm our hearts. A story about how Naomi faced a void, a valley bottom experience-she lost her husband and only sons by the way of the grave. Yet, God did not leave her empty. He had blessed Naomi with two of the most outstanding daughters-in-laws. Especially one whose name was Ruth. She is known throughout history for her classic expression of loyalty and love. Ruth's commitment to her mother-in-law was total, complete, and unconditional. Because of this, this story changed a single woman's desolation and emptiness into fullness and completion.

It's every mother's secret heart's plea to desire her children to be blessed with the best helpmates. As long as I can remember, I too have been asking God daily to orchestrate a perfect match made in heaven for each of our three children. And God is always faithful above and beyond to lend an ear. He loves to move into action and provide "pressed down, shaken together, and running over." Naomi could not have been a more blessed mother-in-law to have Ruth as her daughter-in-law. Yet, I do believe history repeats itself. In this generation, I too am one of the most blessed mother-in-laws to be, three times over.

In this world, so many are without true hope; many do not get to taste true unconditional love. This means to love in spite of flaws and broken communications and shattered expectations. It goes beyond the performance of the other person. Before we can freely receive the savoring flavor of such unconditional love exampled by Ruth, let's lay down our pride and raise up God's gift called love.

Let's sincerely pray this...Please help me, dear Abba Father. I know in my mind what is the noble thing to do. Yet, as You know me well, this is easier said then done. I also know something priceless-*Your purpose is to redeem*. Since this is Your heartbeat, it shall be mine also. I too must join in on the same side as Your team and on the same side of the battle line. I'd fight to love like Ruth loved, like Jesus loved, like You love.

Reflect on Tea Time With Jesus...

BEAUTIFUL CHANGE

...but whoever listens to me (says the Lord) will live safely and be at ease without fear of harm. (Proverbs 1:33)

Look at the great wonders of this world. They are indeed the authentic works of God's hands. It amazes me to see the intricate details God pays such close attention to as He tediously labors on His handiworks. Take the caterpillar, for instance, it is delicate and plain when it first starts off in life's journey. Yet, God cares for it and provides for it every step along the way. It doesn't need to fear from its enemies' strongholds.

One day, when God says "it's time to grow up," it must do so. It must obediently face the greatest challenge of its life. The measly worm enters a season when it must labor like it has never done before. It does not need to fear or fret, because it can totally lean on its Maker. Its Maker has already orchestrated and planned for its success.

He has given it the ability to know exactly how to build its big project, the perfect cocoon. I'm sure there are no Cocoon-Making 101 classes. With each tedious thread woven, the stress level rises also. But the little caterpillar does not give up. He finishes.

At this point, the weary one finds a short resting period. It's a time to stand still and wait. At the perfect moment, God's final instructions come through. The words are, "Go forth." This final stage of obedience is crucial to completing the beautiful change.

Let's say at such a time, a concerned human comes along. He tries to help speed up the process. But this good intention will turn out to be quite devastating. Why? Well, without the struggle, the caterpillar cannot change. Without change, it can't become the beautiful butterfly God planned for it to be.

It's similar in our lives. Count it a blessing when we face struggles. For through the endurance of it we can build strong spiritual muscles. This helps change us from glory to glory into the beautiful masterpieces God has meant for each of us to become after the cocoon stage. So if we are in a season of struggles, don't throw in the towel. Do not look for an easy way out. Do not see it as a bad thing. *It's a blessing in disguise.*

Listen carefully...commit to the Lord whatever you must do. Know beyond a shadow of a doubt, your hard times will eventually blossom into fruitful times. *Catch this*...when you first started off as a green sprout, God already believed in you. He believes in you to become the awesome giant, a major league home runner. Believe in this also, for God is not a liar: Trust in God Who will not ask you to do anything without first providing the answer.

So fasten your eyes on the greatest adventure of a lifetime directed by the best Conductor ever. Take heart in the precious season of growth. A beautiful change waits after the season from caterpillar to butterfly, from ordinary to extraordinary.

THE ROLL CALL

Nothing impure will ever enter it...only those whose names are
written in the Lamb's book of Life. (Revelation 21:27)

Have you ever experienced standing at the end of the line, feeling hopeful that someone might recognize you? Everyone is enthused and confident, everyone except you. One by one the names are called, all the way down to you. Last in line, last to be chosen? I've experienced this in elementary school during P.E. classes. Because I was one of the slowest runners, not an athletic bone in my body, I was the last one chosen. The team captains would have jumped for joy if they could have traded me off to the other team. In Social Studies I was known as the "always a day late" student. Perhaps it was because it took me forever to grasp the truths of history itself. Finally when I did, I was "always a day too late."

There is, however, one date I will with my might be on time for. What is it? Well, when the Roll Call resounds throughout heaven and earth, I don't want to miss it. When God calls out the names recorded since the beginning of time, when the A's through R's are called out, and when God says the names which begins with S's...amongst it, I want to hear...

"Well done, Marcus Sanders"

"Well done, Christopher Sanders"

"Well done, Timothy Sanders"

"Well done, Janell Sanders"

and so many more familiar and precious names. At this Great Roll Call I do not want to be known as the "day-too-late" child. I want to be there on time. In the midst of a history of names, it will mean the world to hear "Well done, Laura Sanders."

Can you feel this too? Lord, You remind me when I see wars and rumors of wars take place, I shouldn't be alarmed. When I see increased wickedness surround me and the love of many grow cold, I don't need to be afraid. For You said to those who stand firm to the end, we will be saved. You tell me, my God, time here on earth is drawing to a close. Soon! I must therefore live life for the reason to meet You Face to face. When You open the Lamb's Book and call out the names at this final Roll Call, help me not to be a moment too late.

Reflect on Tea Time With Jesus...

OPPORTUNITY OF A LIFE TIME

...I press on to take hold of that for which Christ Jesus took hold of

me...I do not consider myself yet to have taken hold of it. But one

thing I do: Forgetting what is behind and straining toward the goal

to win the prize for which God has called me heavenward in Christ

Jesus. (Philippians 3:12,13)

I did not come this far to make a mark on this place called earth. I am not placed here for such a time as this to find fame or fortune. My life's goal and fulfillment is solely dependent on lifting the Name of Jesus. I get to do this with joy as God orchestrates which people I get to cross paths to do life with. And yes, time escapes through our fingers too quickly. So for this moment there is one thing I must choose to do with all I have in me. This means to live out loud this verse: *I press on to take hold of the very reason Jesus took hold of me.*

And what does this take? It will take the same reason God came to earth to redeem your soul and mine. Our souls could have, would have, should have deserved to be lost forever. But because of His love towards you and me, we were rescued. God chose to give His own Life in return to save ours. So then what can we do so we will not waste what God has done for us? We can choose to throw ours across the floor also. No matter if in sickness or in health, at the mountain top seasons or in the valley bottom times, we can live His testimony out loud.

This season, for our household, we face a time of unanswered opportunities. This page holds a definite change in store for us. Timothy, our discerning son, told me "I knew for a while that change was going to happen to our family."

'Change' for me is out of my comfort zone. I love to situate things in their cozy spot. When movement happens, I feel so uncomfortable. Just a few days ago, as my husband and I drove back home, I gingerly said, "Honey, no matter if any tough circumstance comes down on us (this includes change), as long as we get to do it together, I'll be alright." Can we make it? Will there be a happy ending? Well, I don't know what tomorrow will bring. I do know God holds my today. I do know God has promised: Although a thousand may fall at our side, God will uphold us. The days of the blameless are known to the Lord, in times of disaster they will not fall. So, yes, I may stumble, yet I will not fall, my steps will be firm. Even when I was young, and now that I am older, "I've never seen the righteous forsaken or their children lacking."

*This sums it all...*God always provides. He is our God Who loves to protect His children with His life.

Dearest Abba Father, I know I can do all things through You. You are the One Who gives me the strength. Even if it means having to go through the fiery furnace, I know You will be there. I'll be alright. My family will be safe in Your embrace. You will walk through the fire with us. The heat will not touch us because You are with us. Like what took place in His-story when Shadrach, Meshach, and Abednego were thrown into the blazing furnace. The fire's flames itself consumed those who came near. Yet, in the midst of the hottest fire, it was witnessed by man's eyes-there was a fourth. Someone was walking amidst the heat with the three soldiers of God. Who kept Shadrach, Meshach, and Abednego safe without a single hair singed? Indeed, it was the Lord God.

Our story is another Shadrach, Meshach, and Abednego's history in the writing. I give You, my Lord, full permission to be the Author, Chief-Editor, and Publisher of it.

Oh, and P.S. My God, I have to admit, I'm a bit fearful. So please quiet my throbbing heart and my chattering teeth. This way I can hear Your Voice and write the best pages yet to be written. I am ready with pen in hand and eyes fastened to You. I know I have one chance to make it count. Here I am, ready at Your Feet.

TASTER'S CHOICE

Fight the good fight of faith. (1Timothy 6:12)

With age, pickled vegetables take on a wonderful flavor. As stew simmers on the stove for long hours to cook slowly, the taste reaches a savory deliciousness that is accentuated because of this patient process. Only in the ripe, opportune time, a fruit is ready to be enjoyed in its fullest flavor. Isn't it true too with our journey of life? Seasons come and go. But if we rush our pages in the chapter of life, we'll miss God's best. If we quit too soon, we're missing out in the very best.

God encourages us to hold on to the very end to 'fight the good fight of faith'. Here is a story with a happy ending, perfect to drive home the taster's choice: These past several weeks have been quite an exciting yet challenging page for our family. Months prior to this, God was already at work in putting into action His great plan for our family. Take a look at the mother eagle that pricks at her nest when it's time for her baby to fly. Her reason is for the sole reason in making the surroundings uncomfortable so the baby may find encouragement to leave its baby stage and soar to higher grounds. Similarly, our family also faces the little prickling situations amidst the fruitful season we were so in love being in. Yet, God was being the all-knowing Father Eagle and allowed thorns to arise out of our comfortable church nest because He had something greater for us in mind. The thorns came in the form of health issues for both my husband and I. At first, my heart began to race with speeding palpitations. The doctors could not figure out the physical answer. But God was already setting the prelude to an exciting new concerto of our next pages in our lives. God was speaking gingerly still clearly so He can orchestrate the accents of notes and beats in each of our spiritual hearts. His message was "this is the end of one season and the beginning of a new one." So God's instructions were for us to step down from our position as Worship Pastor. It was our time to "rest". At that time, we did not know why, but we stepped forward by faith and chose to obey our God. Our God was indeed a follower of His Words and leader of His actions. He never lets us down. Surely enough, as minutes unfolded into days, we arrived here in our new season. It is a time when we get to taste God's dessert of a new beginning. For over a decade now, we have not taken a breather. Yet it is clear the harvest field is ripe and laborers are much needed in such a time as this. So we will take a short comma in our chapter as a family and prepare to take our grand crescendo into the finale days of this precious season called life. And life we do for the Author of it. No, it will not be a waste; instead, it will be a well in the midst of a desert, a rainbow after the storm.

*Here's a happy ending...*God has taken our household through many seasons. Yet without fail, He takes what seems to be a disaster to man and creates a masterpiece out of it all. I am indeed looking forward to a God-orchestrated new season. As seasons come and go, I know this is just a taste of one...as we continue to fight the good fight of faith. At the end of it all, I hope that I have given all I can with nothing held back. Then after I have spent all, I hope I will have pleased God inside out. I desire my life to have been a sweet aroma to my Lord. For God has indeed been the Delight of my life. He is truly the Taster's Choice. *I love my Tea Time with my Jesus.*

Reflect on Tea Time With Jesus...

CPSIA information can be obtained
at www.ICGtesting.com
Printed in the USA
FSHW012125141118
53810FS

9 781603 830584